Like Sunlight Falling into Water:
Poetics Along the Way to the Horizon

Like Sunlight Falling into Water:
Poetics Along the Way to the Horizon

Charles S. Pinzino

SunlightFalling

Kansas City and Gladstone

Missouri

2019

First edition: 2019

ISBN: 9781091604933

Library of Congress Control Number: 2019903885

Cover Photograph: Gary L. Campbell—*Sunset Afterglow*, taken near Roche Harbor, Washington on the northwest end of San Juan Island.

Dedication

To my closest companions on this journey,
with gratitude for the chance to be here with you in the
midst of all that is, *visibilium omnium et invisibilium.*

Contents

Acknowledgements ix

Preface xi

Air 1

An Editor Retires 2

An Eventful Day 4

April at the Piano 5

Arrival 6

Autumnal 7

Close 8

Cold Syrial 9

Contemplative Postulations 12

Disappointment 14

Dreaming 15

Earth Born(e) 17

Evenings 18

Fall Trees 20

First Friends 21

Forever 23

Free Fall Revisited 24

Fuzzy Logic 26

Giving 27

Going On 28

Haiku 29

Heartlands 44

Heron at Rock Creek Bridge 47

How Death Comes 48

Into the Darkness 50

Inversorial in Times of War 52

Love and Death: A Fantasy 53

Millennium 57

Morning 59

Mountain Memoir 60

Note to Young Pilgrims on the Path 61

On the Same Wind   62
Pilgrims   63
Rain   64
Reflection   65
R.E.M   66
River Afternoon   67
Sand Point Memoir   68
Scene and Unseen   70
Searching for the Secret   84
Seventy   85
Sometimes at Night   86
Song of Native Snow   87
Starlight   89
Stitches in Time   90
The Light Before Christmas   95
The River Bed   98
The Sound   100
The Temper Stone   102
Theory of Everything   106
Thoughts Just Upwind of Spring   107
Travelogue August 2018   108
Triptych in Spring   111
Water   114
Winter Passenger   115
Winter Solstice   116
Yes and No   117

Acknowledgments

I would like to especially thank John Dietz, Laura Luckert, Anthony Glise, Aaron Campbell, Richard Murphy, Karla and Jared Hoffmann, Joseph Davidson, and Beth Omeccne Epperson for their time, thoughtful insights, and encouragement in editing, reviewing, culling, and honing the material for this project. I want to also thank my "first friends", former career colleagues, and family for being there to listen, read, and share at various times and places across the years.

Preface

As the wake of my boat is now much longer than the distance to the horizon, I have felt a need to gather up these writings as part of my legacy for being here.

In looking through folders of what has accumulated over fifty years, some items were associated with a specific person, time, and place and would not translate well to a general audience. The items included here are the best of the rest.

I have decided to present the poems, stories, and reflections in alphabetical order by title rather than by theme, style, or date. As to style, I don't have a set one. How the items appear on the page depended on what felt right in terms of subject matter and flow at the time. I have tried to find the music in words and phrases using alliteration and rhythm when it did not constrain or constrict the thoughts I wanted to convey or force an awkward expression.

Occasionally I have used parentheses to elicit more than one connotation for a thought: e.g., t(here), s(now), e(yes). While this is interesting when reading silently, it does present a challenge when reading aloud as one must choose which word to read, and often the choice gives a subtly different cast to the meaning one takes away.

I initially followed the traditional three-line, 5-7-5 syllables-per-line format for the haiku. I tried to further concentrate the images using 3-5-3 syllable lines. I decided to present both forms, since the condensate sometimes invokes a slightly different feeling.

Under the category "Scene and Unseen" are captions I wrote for some photographs taken by my good friend F. Lee Cornelison—"scene" referring to the visual image in the photograph and "unseen" for what may be visible or inferred only in the mind's eye. I have included them here as an exercise in imagination. The photographs with captions may be viewed at sunlightfalling.com (coming soon).

The book title is derived from images in two poems herein, "Reflection" and "Seventy". It seemed an appropriate metaphor for the sunlight of consciousness interacting with the mysterious waters of the subconscious—the sensate world with the intuitive mind.

Having been an avid reader, it is quite possible I have unintentionally incorporated here or there an image or phrase that drifted down from another author's mind and left an imprint on mine. If so, I hope I have done so in a creative and respectful way. I would gladly acknowledge those mentors should they be made known to me.

Although I have not been a prolific writer, I am grateful the Muses have visited from time to time along the years. Though thoughts and feelings cannot always be expressed adequately in words, I have enjoyed trying to capture and preserve them at various intersections of my own path through life with the world as given. I sincerely hope the time you spend with them turns out to be worthwhile.

Charles S. Pinzino
January 2019

Air

The air is bad today.

Fumes from civilization
exhausting itself
steep like tea
in stagnant humidity,
the breeze so still
leaves dream
of moving by themselves.

On the news
comes the stench
of exploded ordnance
and decomposing corpses
from half a world away.

The air is good today.

An Editor Retires

In the days before delete buttons
you deciphered exquisite scribbles
on hand-written drafts,
the clatter of keystrokes
punctuated by dings
digesting alphabet soup into sentences.

Maimed language lying
on crisp white sheets—
you sustained a human heart sound
within the arcane jargon
of scientifically anesthetized prose
to meet deadlines and rescue dead lines
demanding immediate resuscitation.

Words, fossilized thoughts
in paragraphic strata
needed your careful excavation
to remove clutter and debris,
unearthing an author's intent.

Years go by
In the blink of an eye.

Managing somehow while walls
went up and walls came down
restructured and reorganized
ad infinitum…task forces
teams red and green
proposals spiral bound
laboratory retorts into final reports

SOPs, CVs, and QIPs
and an acronym for every purpose
under heaven.

Will you miss the invigorating odors
of new carpet adhesive
or faint sulfurous fumes
when breathing in the rhapsodies
of wood smoke and sweet grass perfumes?

Will a faint echo linger
of soft keyboard clicks
inscrutable non-computable
chirps and peeps
that queer electronic grunting
during software downloads
and data dumping?

Or will the ghosts of those sounds sleep
through the summer night chorus
of crickets and katydids
or the cawing of crows come autumn?

Closing the office door
one last time,
re-desking yourself
a few clicks to the north
trading mouse pads for field mice
where the grammar of nature
and the serene script of the universe
like ripples on water
or waves across wheat fields
never need editing.

An Eventful Day

"...all things are couched in eagerness
to become something else...." Peter S. Beagle

Morning curved cautiously
Around the contours of the creek
Along the way to afternoon.

Fragments of fog broke free
From dewy hollows,
Angelic transmigrations
Diaphanous in the light
Ascending beyond sight.

A lizard, partially propped up
From the shallows on a stone,
Suddenly shape-shifted into
A protruding stick.

Clouds unfolded into invisibility
And re-cloaked downwind
In new guises while stars hid
Behind the blue breadth of the sky.

A rounded rock, prompted by
Breezes stirring shade to sunlight,
Sprouted legs, neck, and tail,
Transformed into a turtle
Emerging from the muck.

Time traversed the steppingstones
Of the hours, passing unnoticed
Within the familiar flow of the day.

The chafing of dry grasses
Masked the melodious trickling
Of remnant water in a summer
That forgot how to dream the rain.

April at the Piano

On the porch of summer,
the spider, a master at reading vibrations,
tests the tether of its web
fine-tuning string tension,
waiting to feel the joyful song
of struggling prey strained from the wind.

Inside, April at the piano,
fingers fluttering over keys,
transforming ink spots
back into drops of sound,
drops that first condensed
from nebulous swirls
onto mental webs in the heads
of Mozart and Bach, becoming
their sonorous signatures in time—
her fingers probing like hummingbirds
sipping the sweet nectar that still wells up
from the calyx of their imagination.

Sound drops merge into melodies
flowing out through the window screen
washing over the porch
floating among the leaves
and the droning of bees,
mingling with the breeze
in a dance of light and shadow.

April at the piano
like the spider in its web,
a master at sensing vibrations—
she feels what it's like
as Mozart and Bach
born again from her fingers
pluck playfully at the strings
of the spider's web
while sailing on their way
out across the day.

Arrival

An abrupt journey
from the soft warmth
of oblivious darkness
          into
the blazing and jangled
responsibility
of the light—
                    Birth.

Autumnal

While light was leaving
by the Western Gates:
>   processions of clouds
>   through twilight cathedrals
and meditations on the fate of the sun.

It is no secret in the forest:
>   hushed music from
>   hymnals of dying leaves,
the trees ordained as
sacristans to colder winds.

At night the starlight
mingles like incense
in distant sanctuaries—
>   ceremonies in darkness
>   condensing to frost below—
the stillness deep with prophecy
foretelling sacraments of ice and snow.

Not long ago
the journey was warm:
hope was
>   more than emptiness
>   less than love
and autumn the only road
we traveled to winter.

The p(light) of candles
in twilit cathedrals—
ashes of incense
embers of dreams.

Close

cloud
sky

shadow
ground

root
soil

flame
wick

paint
canvas

pen
hand

space
time

ink
paper

thought
mind

Cold Syrial

In the apse of inner silence,
one approaches
the nearness of all distances
and the farness of what is close.

I have
gone there
after the
Aleppo boy
besmirched in
mud and blood
was sat down
dazed in a chair,
ambulanced
after the bombs,
rescued from
a rubble
of
bodies
and stones
in
the ruins
of innocence
and
moral impotence.

I have gone there
after a refugee child
washed up
on the beach
bedded face down
in the wet sand
drowned in a lullaby
of lapping waves,
tossed from a nightmare
we never seem
to wake from.

I have gone there
after the *sarin* fell,
that lovely *sarin*ade
from the bomb bays
of the *sarin*geti planes
bestowing the piece-full
*sarin*ity of dying
a *sarin*dipity-do
of frothing breath
and paralytic pain,
the constricted
convulsive aftermath
of perfidy and
perjured promises.

I have gone there
after the photos
were filed away
and the news crews
along with the outcry
moved on.

que sera sera
nihil obstat
if
the
war
goes on
libera nos
que sera sera

I have gone there
in the outrageous absence
of unmitigated outrage
and approached the nearness
of those distances
and the farness
of what was
all too close

only to hear
the apse collapsing
as I remembered
the painted figure
and heard the scream

Der Schrei der Natur

and
I felt
time
trickling
down
my cheeks
like
tears.

Contemplative Postulations

I.   The process of the soul is fixed within the contingencies of time and space at the moment of conception. Birth isolates the physical manifestation of the soul and exposes the senses to the stimuli of the cosmos permitting the evolution of consciousness. As consciousness matures to self-awareness, responsibility for the further development of the soul is no longer rooted in mere being or passivity, but requires initiative and the active participation of the self.

II.   Destiny is the offspring of two wills—that of fate, the implicit will of the universe as given, and the human will. Life is the dialogue through which these forces communicate with and engage each other seeking equilibrium. Through the resulting dialectic, the coarse matter and energies of the self are refined to spirit and the soul is gathered into the vital stuff of emerging foreverness. Thus the journey procedes.

III.   In the deeper recesses beneath awareness this journey is still coded. Through the processes of living, we embrace it as best we can and become unique pathways for its myriad unfoldings, ultimately responsible for its manifestation and transmission. There is a part of the mystery that can speak only with our voice and be shaped only with our hands.

This mystery does not yield itself passively. Rather, like a wave, it unfolds across the shores of consciousness, a small part of its secret seeping into understanding before washing away with it something of the self as it merges once again with the incessant churning and chaotic obscurity of the subconscious mind.

IV. It is within the flow of loving relationships that we can most fully actuate our own being and establish the dialectic between ourselves and the mystery. Only to the extent that we are loving persons can the mystery become known through us, and the journey decipher itself toward that dark slow flame that kindles everything back to perpetual beginning and rebirth.

V. Within the changing of the seasons and the coursing of our blood, the life-flow is continuous, mediated on the one hand by the ethics of sun and wind and on the other by the rhythmic truth of the heart. In the dark quiet aloneness of the soul one becomes aware that it the nature of the life flow to be transmitted, and that love is the primary medium that allows it to be transmitted freely and without distortion.

Disappointment

Nearing the edge of winter,
a few moments of sun
tragically mistaken.

Warmth.
Stretching and flexing
of the grass.

(Dis, Dis,
What's this, what's this?
She sighs in her sleep.
Plow her while you can.
Climacteric of friction,
the burial of seed.
Love her while you can.)

But the roots were not fooled.
Undisturbed groping
through sedimental darkness,
tactile wisdom slowing the sap
before being spent.

Already see the grass,
re-bent to colder dreams,
marking the path of the passing wind.

Dreaming

De profundis clamavi ad animam hominis.

As the moon rose high
in the evening sky
with the stars like diamonds gleaming,
while the earth turned 'round
came the restless sound
of ten million children dreaming.

Some in slumlord beds,
some with pillowed heads
some with rag wrapped wounds
still seeping.
Some near shopping malls,
some in orphan halls,
heaven's promises lay sleeping.

As the moon sailed on
toward the brink of dawn
the wild heart of life kept beating,
while the waves of war
lapped at every shore
all too frequently repeating.

Who will hold them tight,
who will give them light
for to see through hate's illusion?
Can the wings of love lift them far above
all morality's confusion?

For ten thousand years
still the same dark fears
shroud the wisdom of the ages.
Human history lost in mystery,
lessons smudged on blood-stained pages.

Great religions paled,
fanatic thought prevailed;
sacred truths warped by obsession.
Fearing freedom's breath,
starving souls to death,
cultures blinded by oppression.

As a new day rose
shedding night's worn clothes
all the children were awaking.
Some to beg for bread,
some in homes well fed...
there are choices for the making.

May the balm of peace
cause all wars to cease
so no soldiers will be needed.
May the hands of greed
share with those in need
and true liberty be heeded.

May all children know
what it's like to grow
in a world where life's respected.
And hear lullabies
as they close their eyes
from all ancient strife protected.

As the moon rose high
in the evening sky
with the stars like diamonds gleaming,
while the earth turned 'round
came the restless sound
of ten million children dreaming.

Earth Born(e)

Earth born(e)
we wander the great dark,
tethered to a star.

Of recent nativity into this ancient circling,
we have come to peer with destined eyes
across an abyss of interminable antiquity.

Through our mind's prism,
eternity becomes time—
past, present, and future.

Tides of our consciousness
continually ebb and flow
along the shores of mysteries.

Aided by thought and imagination,
we embellish our dreams
and construct our beliefs
with the few grains of truth
we manage to loosen and carry away.

Tenuous alloys of matter and spirit,
we have disturbed the universe
with appalling nonchalance.

To our knowledge,
we grow out of the only cradle of life
in the cosmos—the first to intrude with
conscience and self-consciousness.

If there is to be a legacy left by our being
to the future unfolding of existence,
let it be the pulse of the human heart
plangent with love, empathy,
and compassion, echoing through
the soundless continuum of space.

Evenings

I

another evening
softly settles
the sun
tracing faint dreams
on the wind

gathering the remnants of day
a few floating colors
finally fade homeward
toward night

darkness
deepens

even(ly)
the silence
shifts

II

evening
the sky is quiet
curtains stir
fragrances murmur
lavender and lilac
tinting the breeze

high up
a full moon
overflows
into after-dusk
unclasping
night's dark robe
inviting nakedness
like the soft insinuation
of a lover's breath
against the skin

III
evening
gray wisps of clouds
float like smoke
aglow against
the tarnished silver disk
of the sun

the air is rain fresh
no breeze
troubles the trees

inverted
a sandglass
makes moments visible
it is not comforting
to see how time
does not
hesitate

the moon's sheen
is now milk white
in high haze
the stars
mostly safe
from gazing

IV
fingers of clouds
enfold a fairytale sunset
riding evening winds
back into eternity's season
fading echoes of light
whisper through wistful fields
beyond the sun's returning
where I might find you
dream-like in soft moonlight
somewhere between your shadow
and my hand

Fall Trees

Fall trees
birth their dying leaves
into the chaotic nursery
of the wind.

I rake the afterbirth
from the lawn
and undertake the grave task
of escorting paper bag coffins
to burial above ground
in the mounded tomb
at the city-sanctioned
yard waste cemetery.

The trees meanwhile
summon sap back down
closer to ground
and nurse dreams
of oozing green in spring.

First Friends

It is quiet now
save for the embers
breathing in the fireplace.
Outside, the winter wind is weaving
filigrees of frost over frozen fields
and tomorrow will be told
in a mosaic of ice and crunchy whiteness.
I sit and watch the fire,
thinking of all the warm things
that have held our times together—

The hours we stirred round and round
in a steaming cup of coffee.

Softer moments we breathed in
and drank while sipping wine.

The walls that felt our shadows playing
gently in the low and easy candlelight.

The laughter we sent tumbling
all over the unsuspecting floor
and the smiles left hanging on the ends
of half-whispered words.

Times when our eyes spoke
in dancing gleams or gentle probings
seeking out the hurt and joy
the aching and pulsing
bittersweet fragileness
that huddled inside
our trembling happiness.

The darkness that moved when it sensed
we sought the secrets of each other's presence,
holding hands, leaning close, side-to side,
hugged and pressed tight.

The rooms that welcomed our songs
and listened until they faded
into a sleepiness of dreamy-tired settlings.

All of that and the love that somehow
snuggled all around everything,
a love that wasn't even all born yet
that sometimes planted promises,
waiting for other springs
beginning over and over
growing because of our meetings
and in spite of our partings
playing hide-and-seek in the midst
of all we did or couldn't do,
all we said or couldn't say.

That half-crazy love waiting impatiently
for the sun to shine silvery
through the clouds
of our misunderstandings.

And so I'm thinking about all this
and it's nearly Christmas
so I think about that too
and about what someone said
a long time ago
about peace
and joy and life
and being together
and most of all
about love.

And because of you,
very much because of you,
I like to tell myself
that maybe I understand
just a little something
of what it's all about.

Forever

I remember
a wedding
once.

There were
a few flowers
and some candles.

The couple
was saying
"forever."

Outside
I heard
the low sobbing
of an air-raid siren
at noon.

Free Fall Revisited

Nudged from my nest
of stressful inertia,
I leap from the ledge, again.
The Sirens' song
seems sweetest nearing Spring.
My airtime will be brief,
like a leaf's letting go.
I test my dream's wings,
trying to forestall my free fall.

It is no use of course.
Though my stomach feels hollow,
I am otherwise too dense for flight.
The interval between my leap
and whatever ground
will be most profound.

      (What madness is this?
      Are there dolphins in our brains?
      Is it some vestige
      of our tails that propels us up
      like whales from brine?
      Some secret clock
      that thrusts us out like cuckoos
      and slams the door behind?)

So quickly life goes by
in the blink of an eye.
Seduced from the safety
of my sleep,
I had to take this leap.

The years fly.
There is no text.
I have to trust what's next.

And when I die,
my life a history of split cocoons
and empty nests,
full of mysteries at best,
even then I will leap down
from beneath the deep dark ground
into the forever after of having been here.

Fuzzy Logic

what has entered
through our senses
    shifts to symbols
    then condenses
to equations formed
in reason's wake
    $m = E/c^2$ [1]

scripting particles
both strange and charmed
    entanglements
    wave distributions
      $S = k(\ln W)$ [2]
uncertainties
 $(\Delta p)(\Delta x) > h/4\pi$ [3]
required exclusions

matter wavers $\lambda = h/mv$ [4]
on a sea
of quantum probabilities
    $H\Psi = E\Psi$ [5]

[1] Albert Einstein:
mass/energy equivalency
[2[Ludwig Boltzmann:
entropy/probability relationship
[3] Werner Heisenberg:
uncertainty principle
[4] Louis-Victor de Broglie:
matter/wave relationship
[5] Erwin Schrödinger:
 time independent wave equation

Giving

Spring brings returning and blossoming;
  these induce Summer.
The gifts of Summer are growth and
   extension; these elicit Autumn.
The gifts of Autumn are harvesting and
   letting go; these invoke Winter.
Winter brings stillness and clarity;
  these restore Spring.

In giving there is transformation.

The ocean releases water, and thus
  the sky knows clouds,
  the mountains are gifted with snow,
  the fields drink rain.
Rivers are born and return the ocean's gift,
blessed and enriched by earth and sky.

In letting go there is harvesting.

When a gift is given, two are received--
one in the heart of the giver.

Treasure all the gifts that return
through the joy of giving.

Going On

The sea goes on and the sea cucumbers and
sea horses and the cuttlefish and crabs
the waves go on and whales and the wind
and the winding rivers they go on
the fir and fig trees and the ferns
and fireflies and the forests go on and
plains and rain and deserts and dunes and
mountains and mist and canyons and
cactuses, jungles and jaguars they go on
the ants and anteaters, bees and butterflies
and hawks and herons and hyenas and
hurricanes, the sky and beyond the sky
go on and planets and plankton and
pumpkins and moons and moon jellies and
meteors and stars and starfish and atoms
and algae and quarks and comets and
quasars and galaxies and gravity and the
universe and space and seasons and tides
and time go on, nights and days and breath
and life and death go on

—sequitur omnia visibilia et invisibilia—

on and on and on and on and on and on
and on and on and on

> without the necessity
> of a
> single
> human
> thought.

Haiku

I

swift bright boiling suns
light years of darkness away
chilly autumn stars

boiling suns
light years of darkness
autumn stars

II

summer evening breeze
window curtains barely stir
clouds expand with ease

clouds inhale
curtains barely stir
evening breeze

III

clouds sailing sea winds
silhouettes of migrant wings
shadows on sundials

clouds sailing
birds migrating south
fleeting time

IV

watching swirling snow
surrendering warm moist breath
window frosting over

watching snow
warm moist breath released
window frost

V

warm mountain cabin
flame footsteps ascending logs
cold night descending

warm cabin
flames rising from logs
cold night falls

VI

above mountain peak
vaporous ground of the sky
cloud exhalations

above us
sky's vaporous ground
clouds exhale

VII

childhood memory
cottonwood cicadas sing
the sound the heat makes

memory
cicadas singing
sound of heat

VIII

lake fog nearing dawn
moon tethering wisps of night
sleepy dreams clinging

lake at dawn
wan moonlight through fog
dreams clinging

IX

moments vanishing
leaving no trail to follow
snowflakes on moist ground

moments gone
leaving no traces
snowflakes melt

X

what did starlight know
arrowing through long eons
no one there to see

stars shining
through countless eons
no one here

XI

spoon stirring warm tea
drowsy reflections mirrored
waiting dreams hover

stirring tea
drowsy reflections
dreams hover

XII

remnants of morning
quietly spilling over
rainy afternoon

morning spills
quietly over
noontime rain

XIII

candle flame flickers
shadows uncloak from darkness
fragile consciousness

candle flickers
wan light in darkness
consciousness

XIV

balloons untethered
multicolored ascension
children sky-painting

colors rise
children's balloons freed
sky-painting

XV

asphalt desert heat
breezes play in sun-drenched trees
lakes of rippling shade

hot pavement
nearby tree shadows
lakes of shade

Heartlands

I

In the blue cold of January,
waiting for the snow.
Wands of afternoon sunlight
through lapses in clouds
glow against the gray horizon.

Later, the soft click of the clock
passing midnight.
The house complains
against the gusting wind.
I listen for the chaotic collisions
of snowflakes muffled against
the window screen,
the regulated click of the clock
against the quiet.
Time like the flying snow
comes and goes
in the blue cold of January.

In San Diego, frost flowers
don't grow on the window.
Waves come and go,
come and go
and there is no snow
save what is remembered
half a continent
and so many seasons ago
driving to the depot
in the dark early morn
on the first day of the year
she should have said no.

II

Spring in the Heartland.
The road winds on past fields
soaking up the sun,
waiting to drink the rain.

Dogwoods and redbuds.
Flower petals
float soundlessly down.
New leaves unfold
high up in trees
against the blue-lit sky.
Perfumes of lilac and sweet grass
intoxicate the breeze.

Driving home
in the Heartland
I think of her
living where the turning earth
sets the sun on the ocean's rim,
and I feel her gaze
resting on the restless sea.

III

Sun-wash over summer fields,
a palette of greens
beneath the blue breadth
of the sky.

Clouds b(loom)
on humid stalks of air
before floating away
like dandelion fluff
on the flowing wind.
Heat and haze,
the highway rolls on.
Moments of a town strewn between
green fields of corn and beans.

Nearing home in the Heartland,
I think of her and am not surprised
when suddenly the wind begins
to smell like the sea.

IV

Autumn in the Heartland.
The last butterflies flutter by
in apple cider sunlight.
Wings row the high seas of the sky
toward temperate harbors to the south.
Crow caws cadence the dwindling chorus
of crickets and cicadas.

On ice fields far to the north
the wind hones its cold blade
waiting to arc down like a scythe
to harvest the season's last warmth.

Past the leafy blizzards of October,
when wood-smoke rhapsodies waft
beneath street lamp moons,
I'll think of her
nestled now in the mountain's lap,
and listen for her heartbeat,
hushed like a lullaby,
sounding for dreams
beneath Montana starlight.

Heron at Rock Creek Bridge

out walking
watching contrails
streak across
the bright blue sky

continuing on my way
lost somewhere
deep in thought
hardly aware
of the trail

until a heron
lost somewhere deep
into stalking the creek
was startled when
I crossed the bridge
(as was I!)
and frantically took flight
along with whatever
I had been thinking

I watched it rising
up over the tree line
it was redemptive
and I felt rectified
like the vanished contrails
absorbed back
into the deep blue
of the sky

How Death Comes

Her arm flails weakly, beckoning.
My sister holding her.
"I can't...breathe...can't...get my...breath."

(Ahab lashed to the white whale,
arm rocked to and fro.
The whale rolling down to the deep.)

In the gray blue cold
of a January morning,
an embolism beached in her lung.
I go for help knowing there is none,
try to give her hope I do not have.
It does not take long.
the grimace, lips receding,
cheeks suddenly sunken,
ashen as an overcast sea.

It was freezing the day we buried her
on the hilltop, next to my grandfather.
Last away as they lowered her down,
I felt the tug of the tide going out,
being over halfway
toward my own departure.

"I'm ninety-eight years old,
and parts just wear out, you know,"
she had said a few days earlier.

And in the dark watch of that night,
her heart listing near thirty beats a minute,
she got up from the hospital bed,
put on her slippers,
and shuffled unsteadily
to the chair where I kept vigil.

Tenderly, she pulled up the blanket
to cover me,
to keep me warm,
to insulate me
from the creeping cold tide
already beginning to lift
and carry her away.

Into the Darkness

'...dream of the dream that never ends...'

I am your broken dream. Help me.
"Go away. I am dreaming a new dream."

Odysseus has smashed upon the rocks
smash smash smash.
He will surely be drowned.
"No, he will go
into the sea to fish."

Men are hollow.
They are blown about
like chafe and straw.
They shatter like crystal.
They scatter like crushed glass.
They are li-
"Go away. I am dreaming a new dream."

I remember a wedding once.
There were a few flowers and a candle.
The couple was saying "forever."
Outside I heard the low sobbing
of an air raid siren at noon.

Once there were roses
when the summer was steadfast.
It is winter. There are still roses.

It is cold. Where will you go?
"Inside."
Will you get a coat?
"No."
Are you afraid?
"Yes."
Why?
"It is dark."

Abraxas is darkness and light
empty and full
bottomless and shallow.
Abraxas is waiting inside.

Smash smash I remember
glass straw chafe rocks
noon then evening
silence sleep.

"Go away. I am dreaming a new dream."

Yes.

Inversorial in Times of War

Peace
Of
Summit
Shimmering
Toward the
Up icy slopes
And press ahead
With the pinions of hope
We secure our lifelines
Of ancient strife
Beneath the glacial grindings
When civilizations shiver
In history's uncertain seasons

Love and Death:
A Fantasy

"The man who lies asleep will never waken fame,
and his desire and all his life drift past him like a dream,
and all the traces of his memory fade from time
like smoke on air, ripples on a stream."   ....Dante Alighieri
                                      Inferno, Canto XXIV

"Venus lies star-struck in her wound
And the sensual ruins make
Seasons over the liquid world,
White springs in the dark."
                                      ....Dylan Thomas

"Venus will not wake you."
                                      ....John D. Dietz

Periodic cries of gulls punctuated the otherwise uninterrupted susurration of the waves. The sinking sun spilled out the last of its life to glow for a few moments on the surface of the sea. Some light escaped into the clouds, but a soft flush of color betrayed its presence, and it was soon coaxed back down and extinguished. Now and then the wind wandered, subdued and silent, attentive to the unfolding twilight.

I sat near the sea's edge, my gaze loosely focused on the horizon. My breathing had become as unhurried as the waves, my mind buoyed in thoughtless contemplation. There was a peace in the simple rhythm of breathing, surrendering and then taking possession of myself, surrendering and then drawing in all things. It was tempting to disappear for a moment at the still point in-between.

A soft after-light lingered on past the sun's setting. Mist began to gather near small coves and inlets farther down the shore. I gradually became aware of a presence approaching. Exhaling everything else and collecting myself with some effort, I blinked my eyes to restore the usual boundaries to things.

Someone was moving toward me from the left. As the distance between us diminished, I perceived the shape of a woman. She appeared to be wearing a clinging diaphanous garment, her hair dark honey-brown, flowing to her waist. I tried to discern her face through the deepening dusk. Amid flashes of recognition, I was disturbed by the thought that hers was more than a face from my dreaming.

As the breeze stirred, her clothing seemed to dissolve, revealing a body lithe and supple, softly curved. By the time she stood before me, I could no longer bring myself to look at her, her presence at once enchanting and bewildering, resonant at the very quick of my being.

After some moments, I felt her eyes pulling at mine, and I raised my gaze to meet hers. Her eyes were alive, translucent, as gray-green as the sea, and I knew who she was. She smiled, reading the recognition in my eyes. "I thought I should find you here," she said, her voice clear and gentle, as liquid as the sea. "After all of your waiting, will you only stare at me?" Her eyes seemed now playful and alluring, almost seductive.

Feeling my chest constrict, I pulled my gaze from hers and sought counsel from the sea. I felt that I wanted to speak. Words came slowly as if from somewhere far away. "I have been waiting for so long...I thought...I thought I held you once, but it was so long ago, so long ago that...that I...."

When I could look at her again, she spoke. "You did hold me once. It was I, but then I could not be for you. Perhaps though you have imagined me near in times of despair. Sometimes as the wind, whispering in your hair. Other times like the sunlight, a warm glow on your skin. Sometimes disguised as a faint fragrance on the evening breeze. Other times as moonlight or night itself as if I had secretly slipped into your dreams and hugged you while you slept, so that you woke with a sweet tiredness, as if you had passed the night in the arms of a lover. When love cannot be one then it is two, for that is the next closest wholeness to one."

As she spoke, an old familiar sadness stirred in me. I sensed that what she said was true. Again I sought counsel with the sea. I felt her eyes pulling and looked up at her.

54

"All that does not matter now," she said softly. "I am here, and I am for you." Her eyes were shy and sensual, almost timid. "Will you not touch me?" she asked. I felt a strange agitation mixing with my sadness. I wanted to lift my hands, but they seemed not to respond. She knelt before me and repeated her question. "You have often used your eyes to touch," she said. "Touch me with your eyes and let your hands follow."

My hand trembled as I reached to touch her. I felt her hair, grazed her cheek, and traced her lips, learning their tactile warmth. When my hand hesitated at her shoulder, she took it in hers and led it to one of her breasts, cupping my fingers around it, pressing against my palm until I knew it pliant and then firm. Looking steadily into my eyes, she drew my hand down along her flank and brought it to rest near the threshold of her mystery.

There came a welling up from deep inside me. I felt it begin to spill in earnest from my eyes. My hand fell away from her. She drew me down, folding me in her embrace, her face against my chest, my tears in her hair.

Waves were searching now far up the beach, slithering around us as she hugged me to her. Perfectly motionless, I felt a lifetime of tension draining away. Where the sadness had been, I felt a space as vast as the sky.

By degrees I became aware of her breathing, waves of warm breath breaking against my chest. My own breathing became reconciled to hers. I felt the waves nudge at us, but when I sought to move, her peace was too deep, her sweetness too clinging. I kept my eyes closed, trying to lock in the warmth and peace. Her heartbeat reached in to slow mine until together they were as one. At times she almost seemed to flutter in my arms, so I pressed her more tightly until I could no longer distinguish her body from my own. It was as if I were asleep, but deeply conscious. I had the sensation of melting, dissolving into some blissful warmth.

I began to feel buoyant, as if sustained on some gentle undulation. It was only when I sought to open my eyes that I sensed the coolness, growing in intensity and yet drifting away from me. My eyes did not respond.

I became aware that my body was sinking away below me, down into the gray-green depths of briny sleep, arms clutched tightly around its chest as if it were hugging someone.

I perceived a rhythmic pressure surrounding me and realized that my consciousness was now a bubble floating on the surface of the sea. After some moments, I sensed palpitations in the air around me.

A beautiful butterfly was hovering nearby, downy, dark honey-brown. On each wing was a large lenticular spot that seemed alive, translucent, grey-green as the sea...and I knew.

My membrane stretched and creaked as she settled. Something descended, probing the thin film of my being. For an instant it was as if I were being drawn up. Then suddenly my space expanded, and I was floating away like breath on the wind, dissipating into a vastness beyond dreaming.

Millennium

The Future slips through
the isthmus of the Present
accumulating as Past.
(The first zero in the second place.)

Patter of raindrops
through Spring green leaves
Summer's humid chorus
of crickets and cicadas
murmurs of wind
in dry Autumn grasses
the soft hush of s(now)
as Winter passes.

The Past,
when remembered,
is re-Present-ed.
(The second zero in the third place.)

Moments,
no matter how beautiful or tragic,
like notes in a song,
must each be released
for the whole melody of a life
to be heard.

When unremembered,
The Past no longer exists;
when not imagined,
neither does the Future.
(The third zero in the fourth place.)

We grow both old and new,
and parcel passing years
into centuries and millennia.

In the first place,
Eternity takes no notice
of these arbitrary notches
we choose to carve
on the imaginary stick of Time.

Unlike starlight falling
imperceptibly down
through the bright blue dome of day,
or the resonance of thunder
high up in cloudy canyons
shaking loose the rain,
the soft click of the clock
passing midnight
has not been here for a thousand
thousand years.

Morning

Morning creeps quietly
to the sill of dreams
dawn pressing lightly
against drawn eye-shades
a flutter from waking.

Waking in the churning
wake of dreams
summoned moth-like
toward brightness
we cling to wings
from night journeys—
mysterious fantasies
of flight dissolving
in clear solutions
of light.

When dreams subside
we reside
hopefully awake
in the residue
called life.

What is left
after the death
of dreams
if we are lucky
is not unkind.

Mountain Memoir

It was Oc(to)(be)r
on the mountain,
seven souls ascending...

a long climb to find
the windy awe of autumn
snow-flanked and relentless
a sensory infusion of wonder.

Some, old
to the newness
others, new
to the oldness
of it all.

Descending
to cabined laughter,
time crackled away
in the fireplace,
hearts w(armed) by
a common h(earth)
of being—
spontaneously simple
simply pro(found)
open to a closeness
close to an openness
at once old friends
and new.

Note to Young Pilgrims on the Path

You have been given a great gift—the gift of life—an opportunity to be here at this time in history, in this place, in the midst all that is, both visible and invisible. Your true task is to live in such a way as to be worthy of this gift. Envisage your gift as a privilege and a responsibility.

There will be times when sacrifice is required. Sometimes a stalemate is as good as it gets. Protect what is most valuable to you. Deploy your resources in a way that allows for mobility, flexibility, and cooperation. Learn at every opportunity.

Choose your confrontations and battles wisely so as not to waste time and energy on what may not be worthy of engagement. Some circumstances may demand risk-taking and boldness, though sometimes advantage is gained by holding firm in the face of provocation.

Anticipate the consequences of your actions. Seek the center within where your conscience resides. Always choose the path with a heart. Do not hesitate to help others on their journeys.

You may choose to yield in a skirmish for the sake of surviving over the long haul. Sometimes refusing what is offered for the taking results in a far more strategic gain. To know depth do not be overly distracted by surface enchantments. Learn to balance immersion and buoyancy, knowledge and intuition.

Pay attention to life with reverence and wonder. Cultivate the virtues of humility, perseverance, compassion, humor, generosity, and honor. Above all, be grateful for the grace of being here.

On the Same Wind

we
have fallen
like leaves

to dance
for a brief moment
on the same wind

for what
ultimate purpose
we may never know

Pilgrims

In the deepest ocean
where no light comes,
life still flourishes and flickers
in the liquid dark.

Seen from this ark of earth,
the fires of a billion suns
glitter—seeds of light
flung far across the fields
of boundless night.

Life and light,
pilgrims passing through
the dark of space-time's arc,
glimmers from eternity
loosed from matter's heart.

Rain

Gazing
out the window
at the gray rain
thinking
that I should be thinking
profound thoughts
though nothing
but muddled somethings
gather like puddles
on a walk,
fogging the window
between me
and the rain.

Reflection

Looking down
seeing the sky
in a pool of melted s(now).

T(here) is a sound
like sunlight
falling into water.

Clouds float like boats
and sink into
the asphalt shore.

R.E.M.

In the transit
of a dream
consciousness
slips out of gear
and time
       for a time
disappears.

Layers of memory
lift away
as sleep completes
the delamination
of the day.

River Afternoon

hours
rinsed with low
and liquid sounds

sunshine
in the script
of shadows

sifting
through afternoon's
drifting rhymes...

the river slows
in secret coves
its well-kept verses
seldom mention

Sand Point Memoir

I stood at the edge of the continent
and gazed long at the sea,
wandered the alembic stench of tidal pools
ripe with the artifices of decay,
and scavenged over driftwood wastes
piled mockingly near the roots
of towering trees.

The shore was a vastness
suffused with sound—
incessant sloshing of water
over rocks and sand,
periodic utterances of gulls and crows,
murmurs of sky and wind.

I witnessed the mercurial rites
of waterfalls splashing down
stony places before vanishing
into the deep mossy green gloom
of the rain forest,
where all light came filtered and dim
through tangled sieves
of leafy limbs and vines.

The fern thickets were close with stillness,
drenched with secrets,
profoundly attentive
to the buzzing of an insect,
the quiver of a leaf,
the twitching of a rabbit's nose.
It was a dense and humid place
of ancient sorceries,
gnarled with enchantment,
rife with the alchemies of vegetation.

I walked the momentarily
abandoned gravel fans
of a wild river,
remembering the beach
where it first tasted salty sand
before surrendering to the sea.

And the waves,
coming and going,
leaving and taking,
merging and submerging....

We touched,
my warmth and their chill.
We met,
they in obedience to their pull
and I to mine.
And we parted,
no longer the same,
but toward the same seeking.

Scene and Unseen

I

Prismatic echoes align
in a slant of autumn sun
descending through dreamy diffusions
to a pool of melted light.

A tinted visage tricked from air
tempts imagination
beyond the lay of leaf and shadow
to theorize the ghostly geometries
of leaves and light.

The art of seeing
is the ability to coax the concealed
from dimensions hidden
amidst the obvious distraction
of what is too readily seen.

II

Clouds collide soundlessly
with mountain crest
rising above forests of frosty green.

Snow harvests
gathered from a night storm
lie stacked along tree limbs,
mounded to vex gravity
and daunt the wind—
cohesions of crystals branching
toward deep blue morning sky.

Wonder accumulates
given the thinnest ledge,
the barest edge
on which to grab hold.

III

A path initials sloping terrain
near a high-ridge summit,
lettering mountains onto mountain turf.

One follows such a path
since there are higher places to be.

IV

An aspen leaf
radiantly transfigured
against the sun becomes
an exploded placenta of light,
revealing luminous layers
of life force, Kirlian-like auras
of incandescent splendor.

V

A pond daydreams,
disguising its depths
by mirroring the sky.

A tree wades,
rooted in its own reflection.

Ripples dissolve distinctions
of color and form,
floating impressionistic images
on fluid canvas.

Water mimics sky:
algaeic clouds moss the horizon.

Surfaces reflect at most angles
and are seldom transparent.

To know depth
we must be willing
to forgo surface enchantments—
temporarily exchanging
buoyancy for immersion.

Truth is often murky,
not fully fathomed
until its habitats
have been sufficiently disturbed.

VI

Wind tumbles down
from the mountain's lap.

Sepia songs of dry grasses
burnish the silence
within an emptiness
full of arrowing sunlight.

We transpose the angles of nature,
dismantling vastness
with walls and fences,
becoming captive,
prey to the wilderness in our own being
until only a withered artifact remains.

VII

A cauldron of flame erupts—
sorcery of fire and moon
mingling in the mind's eye
to conjure a being
from the night's imagination.

In the primeval present,
ancestral archetypes still leap
from the crucible of the subconscious,
companion *dramatis personae*
on our inner journey.

VIII

I remember this magical day
when the clouds came down—
billowing veils of snow
draping the sill of the horizon,
the blustery face of a storm
chiseled from swirling shrouds
of ice, dust, and wind.

An endless procession of snow-cells
paralleled our path,
their present, past, and future
ours in a glance.

Moments of pure grace
in our space
at the bottom of the sky.

IX

Silhouettes and shadows.
Tree limbs and branches
vein the horizon.
Conduits of darkness
through deepening dusk
web the last luminous moments
of light into the embryo of a dream.

X

Aspens and oaks
score the brief interval
before autumn yields to winter
in fugues of color and shade.

The gem-like sun
gleams from leafy settings.

Fall-cloaked forests
will soon be stripped
by the full-bodied wind
while mountain peaks,
now bare breasts of earth,
will shiver beneath
blankets of snow.

XI

You see the silvery surface
of the sea sun-plated imperfectly,
the dark trough of a wave
curling near shore,
whitecaps sudsing over
half-submerged stones,
a pale strand of clouds strung
across the throat of the sky.

Centering, you see
the miniscule sail of a solitary ship
sailing the silvery surface of the sea—
your soul awash with
the immense mystery
of being here.

XII

Backwaters crinkle
like paper lantern patterns
soaking up hues from evening haze
while the sun, saturn-like,
wears a nebulous ring.

Night-black trees fossilize,
embedding in the twilight.

XIII

Swaybacked from decades
of being ridden hard
by wind and weather,
nearly collapsed
from the burdens of an age,
a rickety cabin still houses
a hollowness full of memories.

Long abandoned by those like us
with erratic and complex destinies,
it still provides luxurious shelter
for winged and four-legged creatures
with less complicated needs and fates.

XIV

Through a rift in the weather,
soft light spills long and low
across snow-kept fields
causing blooms of dry grass
to blush with gold.

Somewhere high up
a hawk loops slow circles,
feathers flexing
in the flux of the wind
and eyes a fence post
as perch from which to prey.

Eaten, prey becomes predator.
The mind digests an image
into a poem. Life feeds life.

Searching for the Secret

We dance round in a ring and suppose,
But the Secret sits in the middle and knows.
                                        Robert Frost

the dust of time drifts
through ageless night
between the stars

in subatomic realms of quantum seas
particles and waves shift shapes,
energies flickering between
predictability and uncertainty

molecules move miraculously
in and out of life,
sequences of beads on genetic strands
animating the embroidery of being

chasing light not yet arrived
from still departing sources
perhaps long since extinguished
far back along time's dusty tunnel,

accelerating particles
toward violent collisions
to chart the digitized trails
of ghostly transients
across fields of theory
in chaotic quantum realms,

feeling our way along
helical strands and knots
fingering the genetic
rosary that encodes us,
meditating on new sequences
we pray not to denature the ark
of our most sacred covenant
while searching for the secret
at the beginning end of time's tunnel

Seventy

The wake of the boat
is now much longer
than the distance
to the horizon.

Ripples fan out
across decades
fading from turbulence
toward serenity
and the shores
where I no longer dream.

Longings are no longer,
save for longing to linger
as long as possible,

unanswered questions in tow,

dropping anchor
to drag against time's current
that seems to accelerate
inexorably toward the event horizon,

hastening to haul in and
rescue my catch of memories

before docking at the portal,
arriving cleared for final departure.

Sometimes at Night

Sometimes at night
when the rain comes
a candle is quite enough light
at night the rain is quiet enough
but not quite enough at night
when it's quiet enough sometimes
the rain is not quite enough when
a candle is quite enough light
not quite enough company.

Song of Native Snow

The Voice of the Snow
Is soft in the forest.
The Voice of the Snow
Melting on moist ground,
Slanting on the wind.
The Snow-Voice speaks
In swift swirling shrouds,
Thick and fluffy,
Flocking in the night.

Great Spirit of the North Wind,
        wings of the Snow-Voice,
Spirit brother to the Great West Wind
        who keeps the sleeping sun,
Your breath stills the face
        of the winding river;
Running waters murmur
        beneath ice stone.

The Voice of the Snow
Floats in the forest.
The Voice of the Snow
Drifts in deep white stillness,
Perching on the boughs of the pine,
Clinging to the cloak of the fir.
The Snow-Voice buries the trail of the deer
And hushes the harsh thunder
Of the wild horses hooves.

Great Spirit Father of the Sky,
        camping place of the winds,
Endless prairie of the rolling clouds,
        bright pasture of the morning sun,
You hide the star fires
        with your smoke-gray blanket,
Your night face hidden
        by cloud and mist,
The tents of the Snow-Voice.

The Voice of the Snow
Dances on the door-skin
Of the dreaming sun,
Touches the tepee of the East Wind,
Laughs in the light of the pale morning fire.

Great Life Spirit, our forefathers sleep
      in your Earth Mother heart,
Their spirits kindle a hearth fire
      in the hearts of our children.
It is your Death Brother who speaks
      with the drums of darkness,
Painting his face
      with the shadow of night.
Together you sew and winnow
      the souls of humankind,
His moccasins dancing the death wish
      in your red life dust.

The Voice of the Great Spirit
Rides on the breath of the wind,
Speaks with the tongue
Of the running waters.
With the Snow-Voice
It speaks a colder truth.

Starlight

If light is
the thought
of stars—

What did
the starlight know
arrowing through
the long millennia
before anyone
was t(here)
to see?

Stitches in Time

We were late away on our annual pilgrimage to the southern Colorado mountains that year. With our jeep in tow, we loaded the pick-up and headed out under the gathering grayness of an early November afternoon. Our route would take us from the plains of Pampa angling the Texas panhandle roughly northwest through Borger and Stinnett, edging the caprock country toward Dumas and Dalhart, before eventually crossing into New Mexico.

We affectionately referred to the highway from Clayton to Raton as the "abomination of desolation". In previous years, we would time our departure to transit this stretch in the wee dark hours of the morning so as to arrive atop Raton Pass in time to witness the sunrise. I remember one year the light of a full moon added an extra veneer of eeriness to the ninety-mile winding route near Rabbit Ears, around Mount Capulin and through the foreboding yet enchanting landscape of abandoned volcanic cones and mounds. But I digress.

At Raton we picked up I-25 to Trinidad, then headed west on CO 12 along the Purgatorie River. By now night had set in and it was starting to snow. Our route turned north at Stonewall passing Monument Lake, and then took us up to Cuchara and the Yellow Pine Guest Ranch—elevation 8500 ft.

We arrived at our "bunk house", unloaded the gear and supplies, and started a fire in the Franklin stove. While preparing supper, my two companions related stories of a previous journey to the mountains, and waking up to snow drifts as high as the roof eaves. That night, in the warm afterglow of fellowship, I lay snuggled in my sleeping bag, listening to the soughing of the wind in the pines while time crackled away in the stove.

Our agenda for these trips largely depended on the weather. To accommodate the different preferences and personalities of those involved, there was not always an established script. Usually if the morrow dawned clear, we would drive up another two thousand feet to Bear and Blue lakes and hike around to acclimate ourselves to the higher elevation. The following day we would climb to the 13,000-14,000 ft. ridge summit near Trinchera peak, either following the stream and watershed up through the forest to timberline, or hiking the old switch-back logging trail. Fortunately, both routes were negotiable with the aid of a stout walking stick. It was not unusual to see the tracks of the clawed and hooved now and then along the route, reminders that we were only visitors in this domain. Even though I'd always briefly rebelled at putting myself through the ardors and resultant aches and pains of the ascent, the experience of achieving the summit and the breathtaking view more than compensated for my discomfort. And besides, I'd remind myself such ascents are spiritual as well as physical, and we do such things because there are higher places to be.

The view from the cabin porch the next morning was like an enchantment. The sky was mostly clear, with a stray cloud or two colliding soundlessly with the mountain crest that rose above a forest of frosty green. Three or four inches of snow had fallen during the night. Evidently the wind had calmed and the tree limbs near the cabin bore neat mounds of harvested snow while branching toward the deep blue of the morning sky. We decided to take the jeep and head up the highway a few miles to La Veta for breakfast. It would give us a chance to check the driving conditions and see if the lakes would be accessible. We felt a wild joy and excitement, grateful for the grace of being in the midst of it all.

The road was somewhat snow-packed from earlier traffic but passable, even a bit slushy in spots. As we cautiously rounded a shaded outcrop we suddenly hit a patch of ice hidden under loose snow. The jeep spun around several times and flipped over into some brush just past the rock face. There were some moments of stunned silence and then we were calling out to see if everyone was all right. I had been riding shotgun but ended up in the back behind the driver's seat. I do not recall the trajectories of my two companions, but both were uninjured.

As I climbed out of the jeep, I noticed that the top of my head felt wet. Evidently I had cut it on the dome light fixture on my way to the back seat. So there we stood trying to assess our situation as I was pressing a handkerchief atop my head to stem the bleeding. Fortunately another vehicle came by and the occupant, a local, offered assistance.

I was dropped off at a home first aid station suited for just such a predicament. As I was being tended to, the local motorist dropped my friends at the nearest service station where they could arrange for the jeep to be towed and assessed for drivability. My diagnosis was a scalp cut, not too deep, that would have a tendency to bleed as most scalp cuts do. After getting the bleeding stopped and applying some disinfectant salve, I was taken to the service station to rejoin my friends. The jeep had arrived and was being checked out. While we were discussing this unexpected interruption in our plans, my head started to bleed again. It seemed like a trip to the nearest ER and a couple of stitches would be inevitable to prevent this from being a nuisance the rest of the trip.

A gentleman who had just walked in to pay for gas noticed my bloody handkerchief and inquired as to what had happened. He said his friend, a doctor, was in the car and that I should walk over and let him take a look. The doc commented that he'd seen many of these types of cuts (comforting words for sure). He then took some strands of hair on either side of the cut in a couple of places and tied them together. He said that would keep the wound closed and allow some clotting to take place. When he found out where we were staying, he said he had a ranch nearby and that he could put in a couple of stitches if we wanted to stop by after the jeep got checked out.

The jeep was deemed safe and drivable for short distances. The road had improved considerably from earlier in the day. We made it to the ranch house and after some conversation and a beer, the good doctor brought out his worn black bag and unfolded an amazing display of various hooked and straight needles. I wanted to ask what he might use some of them for, but thought better of it. While my friends kept me distracted with some humorous comments, the doc snipped off the hair knots, applied some local anesthetic, and deftly sutured up my cut.

On the way back to the cabin somberness seemed to settled over us much like the gray cloud cover beginning to blanket the sky. The mountain peaks on the high ridge loomed like bare knuckles on a clenched hand. We rustled up a bite to eat, and did hike a bit in pairs or alone up behind the cabin in the surrounding foothills. Mostly the air had gone out of our adventure-seeking balloon. I think we began to reckon with what almost happened to us if we would have collided with the rock face rather than landing in the cushioning brush or if there had been oncoming traffic.

On toward evening we walked down to Cuchara and dropped in to see the cabin owners whom we had gotten to know on previous visits. They inquired about our day's activities and we recounted what had transpired. When we related our good fortune of meeting the doctor at the service station, and the "stitches in time" at his ranch house they started to laugh. "Yes," they said, "the doc has a practice in Denver and spends time out here on weekends and whenever he can get away. He's very experienced and knows a trick or two, shall we say, like tying that cut closed with your hair. We've heard of him doing it before, but you might be the first person he's ever had to do it on. I guess in a way you were 'out in the field' which is where he usually gets called to in an emergency. He's a veterinarian!"

The good-natured mirth of that revelation dimmed later with the embers in the stove as I lay thinking that night. My friends had wives at home and one had children. Precious time with them was sacrificed to allow for our pilgrimages to the high places. The responsibilities of having a family makes one more conscious of what can be at risk. During the afternoon, I had sensed their thoughts turning back in that direction more and more, which was quite understandable. So in the morning without much being said, we just started packing up to head home.

A week later I was back in the doctor's office to get my stitches out. The nurse remarked that whomever had done the stitching had done a fine job, though the suture thread seemed a bit coarse. I smiled and told her I was just glad the doc wasn't just horsing around.

I think we all have our appointments with fate. The natural world is sublimely indifferent to us though we are part of it, despite its transcendent and inspirational beauty. We are lured and summoned through a web of relationships and chosen paths to places and events that have the potential for unanticipated adventure or perilous outcomes, both physical and spiritual. Whether we find unexpected treasure or simply the good fortune of survival, it is with a sense of gratitude that we should undertake the task of passing on the stories.

The Light Before Christmas

Christmas Eve arrived dank and gray, not unusual for a shallow-lit day just past the solstice. I was not in a particularly festive mood, beset by a list of last minute errands and having to scurry around in the dreary weather. I returned home in the late afternoon to find a parcel on the sodden porch. Not expecting anything, I looked to see if perhaps it had been delivered to the wrong house. The package bore no name or address.

Once inside, I removed the brown outer paper to find a nicely wrapped box with a tag saying "from Santa". My gift turned out to be a Himalayan salt lamp. There was a hand-printed note explaining that it was to be placed in a room near books. I immediately began to narrow the list of culprits and soon arrived at two possible Santa suspects, both of which were my nieces and godchildren. Over the years I had taken them and then their children for "adventures" in the outdoors or at museums and they were familiar with my home and office. The gift implied a familiarity with my fondness for the natural world and for books and reading. Now I had to devise a plan to reveal the giver.

Since I would see them on Christmas day at the family gathering, I decided to concoct a tall tale about the condition of the package when I picked it up and then read their facial expressions, confident it would be easy to discern the guilty party. I would relate that I had found a package upon returning home, but squirrels had investigated it first and chewed through the wrapping in several places. Furthermore, the contents had gotten rain-soaked, and the salt dome had partly dissolved away.

The first suspect arrived at the gathering with her husband and two girls. I was helping them with their coats when her 8-year-old daughter tugged on my sleeve and asked with a big smile on her face "Did Santa bring you any presents, Uncle Chasie?" Wow, I thought, there was no doubt who my secret Santa was. However, I decided to proceed with my plan. As I recounted finding the squirrel-chewed, rain-soaked package, she began to shift uneasily and her face took on a very forlorn look. I realized it was not wise to continue the ruse, and admitted that I was just joking. I told her I had indeed found this wonderful present on my doorstep in good shape, and that the warm orange glow of the salt lamp was at this very minute shining atop the bookcase in my spare room office. The smile returned to her face.

Later, her mother pulled me aside and said there was a bit more to the story of how this all came to be. Evidently, this was the year that her daughter found out who "Santa" really was. Some kids at school had told her it was all make believe and there wasn't a real Santa Claus. Being a very forthright child, she promptly confronted her parents and demanded the truth. When they confessed, she was beside herself at having been "fooled and lied to" by her parents and became almost inconsolable. The best efforts of her father held no magic for this predicament. Finally, her mother was compelled to reveal another secret to help her understand a more grown-up conception of Santa and gifting.

My niece and I had for many years enacted our own version of Santa at Christmastime. I would save a sum of money and then give it to her. It was her job to choose how to use the money and on whom to spend it, the only conditions being anonymity and helping someone in need. My niece told her daughter some of the Santa things we had done, and explained that she was now old enough to be in on the secret and could be a Santa herself. That seemed to turn the tide. Ironically, I had been chosen to be the recipient of her first grown-up secret Santa adventure.

I would never have concocted the damaged package narrative as a test had I an inkling my secret Santa was a child. It had been a bit cruel and almost spoiled the joy of one so excited to participate in such a loving gesture for the first time. As she grows up, she will come to understand that gifts appearing on Christmas morning have little to do with naughty or nice lists that Santa keeps or behavior reports from elves spying from shelves. Rather, they are given simply and profoundly because she is loved.

As I recover this memory, the warm, orange glow of the lamp still emanates from atop a bookcase near my desk. I am reminded that even in dank and dreary times, a bit of light and warmth might arrive in the most unexpected way, perhaps borne by the most innocent of hands. After all, legends tell of another child who came bearing a gift of light to show us the way to live with each other. And whether or not the ion field supposedly generated by the lamp enhances creativity and a sense of well being as the printed instructions claim, I cannot say. But now and then when the weather is rather foul and dreary in my soul, I remember how a light came to me unexpectedly once before a Christmas, and opening that gift warms my heart again.

The River Bed

Along the dunes dervish winds
mimic graver demons.
Invisibilities spiral into dust
on August afternoons.

Dry sandy time
flows through the riverbed,
dry sandy time leaving behind
stones that surface or sink,
eddying currents of wind in the dust,
and bones, rooted in the dust,
bleached bones that gleam
when lizards crawl by moonlight
while owls flex feathers in the dusk,
bones once fleshed from grass
that rooted in the dust.

The past is just beneath
where the present drifts.
The past is next where the present erodes.
The past will be presently future
when the surface erodes.

It is all still here but not still—
a place in time
a moment of space
in motion at the interface….

And now it's midsummer
when dragonflies dart
and heat warps the air
while dying insects
savagely wing the sand,
and something is here
something is here that knows
the water that was here long ago.

"Who is that owl?"
who-whooo-oo-who
"Who is that owl?" a shaman said
casting bones on the riverbed,
and the future gleamed by moonlight.

Dying is not easy when it is not the end.
Death is not for some
when life is as music to the deaf for some.
Dying is not the end…

blood crusts in my veins
my eyes still as stones basting in the glare
lungs sear laboring like billows
skin begins to craze and flake
my heart pumps dust through dry canals
static crackles along nerves
sparks arc synapses
muscles shrivel
tendons twitch and snap
heat beats down baking my bones
my skull a furnace
memories of moisture run hissing
through sizzling coils in my brain
and explode like resin from a flaming log
all thought desiccating to ash….

I fell asleep to the music of water
vanished from time
to some more ancient way--
monks chanting vespers
at dusk in cathedrals,
a sage counting sticks
by a stream in Cathay.

Dreams guard the threshold.
The portals are within.
Invisible generations spawn
in shrouds of dust and sleep.

The Sound

I

Somewhat north of the canyon
a farmhouse on the Texas plains
a row of cottonwood trees
along the eastern side.
All night long there was a sound
saturating her childhood memories
of stifling summer evenings
the bedroom shared with her sister,
all the windows open,
she could hear "the heat,"
cicadas singing in the cottonwoods...
... even late afternoons and evenings,
relentless on those still warm nights
while in her bed restless
waiting to sleep and dream
there was that sound...

II

The wind blew the years on south
to a city far from the farm
two children of her own now grown
and all the while something else
a different heat grown rogue within
making no sound, eating away at her
until a late spring day
that brought her to her dying,
her mother at her bedside,
the bedroom window open,
she was looking through it...
...cicadas were making that sound
the sound that would carry on
through the coming summer
and all the summers
she would never know...
through the open window
she could hear it....

The sound coming to her
laden with memory,
a flash of feverish lucidity
carrying her back to the farm,
to that shared room from childhood
with her sister, not knowing then
her sister would be following
all too soon, too soon....

And of all things
that should not be left unsaid
as she waited to dream no more...
(through the open window she hears it)

"Mother....Listen...the heat..."
nearly her last words...spoken.

The Temper Stone

The occasion was a family gathering at the home on Ashland Avenue in St. Joseph, Missouri we mostly grew up in, affectionately referred to as "Ashland house". Some of us had only sort of grown up, but still managed to have careers nonetheless and even children of our own.

On this particular occasion, I was out exploring the neighborhood with one of my nephews. He was in the midst of grade school, insistent on the time-wasting propensities of homework, and displaying a bit of an edgy attitude.

So, this Sunday afternoon found us walking alongside the stone wall on down the block from the house. This wall was a hallowed location for certain rites of passage that all young nieces and nephews (eight in all) were expected to negotiate. The first challenge was to be lifted up with a little coaxing and a lot of trepidation to stand on the top. Once that had been mastered, the next phase involved walking the top while holding the hand of the accompanying adult, and (this is important) consenting to be hoisted down usually after several round trips. Kids as you know are wont to endlessly repeat new learned skills even if a bit scary, and adult support arms do after all get fatigued. The final test was walking the wall without support, and finding the courage to jump down without assistance. This nephew had already passed the wall initiation with flying colors.

In the course of our walk, the conversation touched on what had impressed him during a recent overnight stay at my house, things such as lighting "those little incense cones", the possibility of dragons, and "it sure is quiet in here" (since I did not in those years own a television). Eventually we returned to everyday chit chat and it was then he admitted that he had been getting into trouble at school. Some kids did or said things that made him mad, and his temper took over and got him into fights.

To properly appreciate what comes next one must understand that this took place in a decade when "New Age" philosophy was all the rage—crystals, vibrations, energy centers, chakras, auras, pyramid power, astrology, aroma therapy, meditation, etc., sort of like the 60s redux. As a scientist, I understood that the energy spectrum of nature was very broad, and that we humans were physically equipped to detect only a very narrow range of those vibrations. There are all sorts of mysterious energy fields and forces that are not well understood, though some people seem to have a built-in antenna for them, like dousers who can find deep underground water with a y-shaped tree branch. Also, I had just finished reading "Even a Stone Can Be a Teacher" (Sheldon Kopp). And finally, I took my role as a trusted uncle and confidant seriously, and in the parlance of the day, I wanted help this child channel the negative energy of anger into something more constructive than fighting.

We talked about how it was all right to be angry and upset, but that the trick was to learn to "let go of it" (fatal choice of words as it turns out). I thought about stones being teachers and energy vibrations. I told him that certain rocks and minerals were believed to have magical properties and could be used to soak up and trap negative energies like anger. He was intrigued. We set off to find a "temper stone" that he could carry in his pocket. That way, when he felt himself getting angry, he could reach in his pocket, wrap his hand around it, squeeze hard, and let the stone soak up his anger. I reckoned it would help him stay calm and keep his temper in check. I told him he would recognize the stone when he found it, but that really, it would find him. He seemed mesmerized by this idea and took to the search with abandon.

All in good time, we happened upon the appropriate stone. It had some glittery inclusions that sparkled in the afternoon sunlight and was of a size and heft that could be easily carried in a pocket and clutched in a small fist.

I told him it would be a good idea to leave it out in the sunshine for an hour or so once in a while. The energy in the sunlight would make the atoms in the stone vibrate and clean out any negative anger energy it had soaked up. It was to be our secret.

Of course, I was feeling quite good about this—glad that I had thought of it and happy he had bought into it with such enthusiasm. I anticipated that his eager attitude and the diversionary "magic" of the stone would indeed buffer his anger long enough so that he wouldn't get into trouble.

Some months later the family was gathered again at Ashland house. It was fall and the overarching maples had dropped a red-orange covering over the lawns and sidewalks. I invited my nephew out for another stroll. Soon we were both kicking through the leafy ground cover, he somewhat more vigorously than I. We talked about Halloween and pumpkins, and how trees let go of their leaves to be recycled so new ones could grow in the spring. I always liked to get a little nature wisdom in when I had a chance.

We crunched on through the leaves awhile in silence and then he said: "Uncle Chasie, we need to find me a new temper stone." I asked him if it had stopped working or if he had lost it. "No", he said emphatically. "Last week at recess this kid made me so mad that I reached into my pocket, grabbed out the stone, and threw it at him!" I did not probe further as to whether harm had been done other than the blow to my ego. So much for my ill-conceived anger management strategy, I thought. Instead of short-circuiting his anger, I had inadvertently provided him a weapon for it.

As I reflected on this memory over the years I came to understand the importance of thinking things through to their logical conclusion and trying to anticipate possible outcomes before prescribing a course of action. Such analysis would be useful in international conflicts where there are larger and far more lethal stones in pockets to be hurled.

After fifty-five years, we moved our parents out of Ashland house and it passed on to a new family. The maples dutifully still let go their colored leaves to fly every autumn. Whether or not the wall down the block is still a rite of passage for other children on the way to adulthood I do not know. My nephew survived grade school and, evidently, so did his recess mates as I did not hear of any new incidents involving flung projectiles or playground injuries. He eventually outgrew the fascination of lighting incense cones and believing in the possibility of dragons, but he did maintain a healthy respect for the wonders of the natural world.

Often when I am out walking and a particular glint from the ground catches my eye, I am reminded about the lessons that can be learned from stones. It's acceptable and perhaps appropriate to pick them up and marvel at the geological journeys that formed and deposited them along our path. After all, they possess an older and far more enduring memory than ours. But mostly it's best to set them back down to be discovered and wondered about in a future age when hopefully, as a species, we will have evolved beyond the need to throw stones, small or large, at anyone.

Theory of Everything

why, when
where—how
did energy first matter?

it doesn't really matter
or
does it?

well…

there were forces
to be reckoned with

and
the gravity
of the situation

so
energy mattered

not hardly at first

but soon
it was elemental

and now
in time

here we are

in light
of everything

still
in the dark…

but that's
another matter!

Thoughts Just Upwind of Spring

The first warmth is only a trickster and not to be trusted. After untold rounds of seasons, roots should be wiser. But every year near the frayed edges of winter, a little warmth seeps down and gets the sap stirring toward buds and greening things. Then, just as there is a bit of cautious peeking above the soil to taste the light, winter feigns recovery. The new growth extensions, manifestations of rebirth, are shocked and wither back to earth, victims of a genetic susceptibility to thermal gradients.

The setback is only temporary of course, but cruel nonetheless, overcoming the long, slow dying down of autumn and the stasis of winter only to emerge and be bent back to colder dreams.

Many plants are perennial, going about life dormant or active as the seasons demand. Others do in truth die, but not before leavings seeds, arks of potential, hoping to be coaxed into growth given the proper environmental embrace.

We, too, sink roots down into the ground of being and grow upward to savor the light, absorbing sustenance from each so as to reach further into the other. After our allotted time, we may truly die, seed a new generation, or perhaps pass through the dormancy of death to re-emerge in the next realm of light.

Travelogue August 2018

We were seven days afloat
in friendships of fifty years
boating around Puget Sound.

Shilshole-Seattle to Poulsbo,
back to Bell Marina and
blooms of Chihuly glass
gracefully aglow
in sunlit gardens,
then up to Kingston,
and across to Oak Harbor.

We did not contest the point
at Point No Point
and passed undeceived
through Deception Pass,
straight across the strait
to the San Juans
and a Monday fuel stop
in Friday Harbor.

Our captain, a skilled
and seasoned seaman,
deftly handled the ship,
charted us along sea lanes,
and made sure the sea floor
remained a safe distance
below the props, angled through
tidal rips and barge wakes,
and orchestrated a ballet
of bow thruster blasts
and engine reversals
while docking us neatly
into our nightly slip.

Along the way
a king salmon
and two crabs,
lured to a meal,
fell for our bait
and were swiftly dispatched
to grace our plates.

The setting sun sometimes
looked like a pastel Necco wafer,
and slipped peacefully into
the watch-pocket-seam of the sky,
or fanned fiery embers
strewn across flowing cloud flights,
the floating watercolors fading
in the pacific afterglow.

At dawn on the final day
morning shrugged off
the last of night's enchantments,
put a few lingering stars to bed,
and followed the sun
over the horizon.

It all begins, they say,
with journeying.
We had arrived across
so many decades
by kindred yet diverse paths
only to depart, once again
homeward bound, with
Port Townsend in our wake.

I had watched the water surface
ripple and churn, and ridden
the undulant buoyancy of the sea
insulated by the hull of the ship.

I have remained
adrift in those days,
trying to fathom
the ineffable sweetness
of wild blackberries,
and the vexing complexity
in the textures of water
I did not touch.

Triptych in Spring

I

Upwind of summer
In the ebbing springtime
On my balcony
      leafing through the
      leavings of another mind
Aware around the margins
      of twilight settling in
The quieting of bird songs
The reflective stillness of a pond

     Time passed…

A solitary insect's
      undulant trilling,
      melodic but melancholy

A questioning,
      hesitant at first,
      repeated,
Becoming more persistent

The intervals shortening,
Asking long past the first star…

     It was alone.
 Darkness was closing…

The only sound it could make…

There was no answer.
     And soon… no question.

II

Upwind of summer
In the ebbing springtime
On my balcony
     leafing through the
     leavings of another mind
Aware around the margins
     of twilight settling in
The quieting of bird songs
The reflective stillness of a pond

     Time passed…

A solitary insect's
     undulant trilling,
     melodic but melancholy

A questioning,
     hesitant at first,
     repeated,
The intervals shortening

The only sound it could make
     becoming more persistent

Asking long past the first star…

     It was alone
and darkness was closing …

Then faintly,
     from a distance,
     an answer.

And soon, the answerer as
     insistent as the questioner.
A brief but frantic dialogue…

And then… no question, and no answer.

III
Upwind of summer
In the ebbing springtime
On my balcony
        leafing through the
        leavings of another mind
Aware around the margins
        of twilight settling in
The quieting of bird songs
The reflective stillness of a pond

Time passes…

Alone
with darkness closing.

A question…

Peering into the distance,
listening long past the first star,
        and wondering…

…Answer or no answer…?

Content and at ease
        either way

Alone

In that enigmatic silence.

Water

The journeys of water
are strange.

At times fluid and sinuous
or invisible, tucked in the folds
of the wind.

There is a wisdom in water—
      freezing, it survives winter
      melting, it accompanies spring
      evaporating, it ascends unseen
      condensing, it clings to itself
      yielding, it surrounds
      merging with cells,
      it escapes briefly into life.

To endure,
a soul must have
the same protean resilience as water,
becoming as liquid, crystal, or vapor
as the seasons of a life demand.

Winter Passenger

Winter wonder of clouds gray-white,
the sun a hazy finger-painted dab
on dappled sky canvas.

Wan silken silver light,
ice cube colored day.
Winds slice through trees
too frozen to bend.

Frigid countryside,
frosty snow patches hide
among rocks on hillsides.
Icicles grown from roadside cliffs,
stayed by the blustery breath
of this slumbering season.

Creeks now glassy highways
opaque and winding.
Underneath, the water whispers—
shadowy shapes glide silently
beneath the frosted glaze above.

All this from the car window,
scanning the land
with seventy-mile-an-hour glances,
thinking of the countless eyes
that have queried this land before,
looking for life
refrigerated in fields
of echoed light.

Winter Solstice

Somewhere,
adrift in a dream,
an echo
of soundless snowfall.

The soul
sips wonder
from a steaming cup
and listens for it

soft as a deer's shadow
gliding on moonlit snow

somewhere in a dream.

Yes and No

sleeping,
the songs
of dreams
why
because
they are
not yet
or
even
maybe
as
she sits
in the
stairways
of your mind
waiting
for you
to say
yes or no
but
you just
watch
because
you
just don't
know
while
her
e(yes)
and
no

About the Author

A native of St. Joseph, Missouri, Charlie has a BA in Theology from Christian Brothers University in Memphis and an A.C.S certified BS in Chemistry from Rockhurst University in Kansas City. He is a retired research chemist (MRIGlobal), and folk guitarist. He has performed and recorded extensively with hammer dulcimer player and Missouri Music Hall of Fame member Esther Kreek. He currently resides in Gladstone, MO.